D0325882

OPEN YOUR MIND,
OPEN YOUR LIFE

Open Your Mind, Open Your Life

A BOOK OF EASTERN WISDOM

TARO GOLD

Andrews McMeel Publishing

Kansas City

Open Your Mind, Open Your Life:
A Book of Eastern Wisdom

03 04 05 06 TWP 10 9 8 7 6 5 4 3 2

Library of Congress Cataloging-in-Publication Data:

Gold, Taro.
    Open your mind, open your life : a book of Eastern wisdom / Taro Gold.
        p. cm.
    ISBN 0-7407-2710-9
    1. Philosophy, Asian—Quotations, maxims, etc. I. Title.
B121 .G65 2002
181—dc21

2002020800

Book design by Holly Camerlinck
Illustrations by Matthew Taylor

With deepest
appreciation to
my mother, Carol,
for showing me
the beauty of
an open mind

PREFACE

For what purpose should one cultivate wisdom?
May you always ask yourself this question.

This simple yet profound sentiment is engraved at Soka University of Tokyo, one of Asia's leading centers of learning. A message to students by Dr. Daisaku Ikeda, an educator and Buddhist philosopher, it perfectly captures the spirit of *Open Your Mind, Open Your Life*.

Our answers to this question, all uniquely personal, reveal our common desire to be happy. I originally wrote *Open Your Mind, Open Your Life* with this perspective—and was soon humbled to see it celebrated as an oasis of advice and insight on our shared journey to lasting happiness.

Building upon that valued tradition, this new and expanded volume of *Open Your Mind, Open Your Life* continues to illuminate life's path with more than 300 inspiring guideposts based on the timeless wisdom of Eastern thought. Readers who treasure the smaller version of *Open Your Mind, Open Your Life* will be happy to find most of the material here is new, while some is shared with the smaller edition. It is my sincere hope that both volumes will continue to encourage without end.

—Taro Gold

INTRODUCTION

THOUGHT CREATES REALITY . . .

Everything humanity has ever created began with a thought. The place where you live, the clothes that you wear, and the paper on which these words are written were once only thoughts in someone's mind. Your decision to read this, too, began with a thought.

HAPPINESS SHAPES THOUGHT . . .

Everything we think is colored by our happiness, or lack thereof. Although individual definitions of happiness vary greatly, we all want to be happy. Early in life, we look for happiness among family, friends, even toys. Later in life, we may look for happiness in religion, money, sex, alcohol, education, marriage. . . . We all know where we have looked. But did we find what we were searching for?

OPENNESS MANIFESTS HAPPINESS . . .

Genuine happiness, or enlightenment, is already within us; we have only to reveal it. As spring water rushes through open earth, so happiness flows through open lives. The question is how to open our lives to this inherent joy. The following pages hold answers to that question, thought by thought, from an Eastern perspective. Most of them may be new to you, some may seem like common sense (which is *not* so common), and others are universal truths not unique to the East. May each of them promote lasting happiness and ways of thinking that truly open your life.

*T*rue happiness in life
is found always within.

■

*S*eek to learn something
from everyone you encounter.

■

*I*f you want to have what you have not,
you must do what you do not.

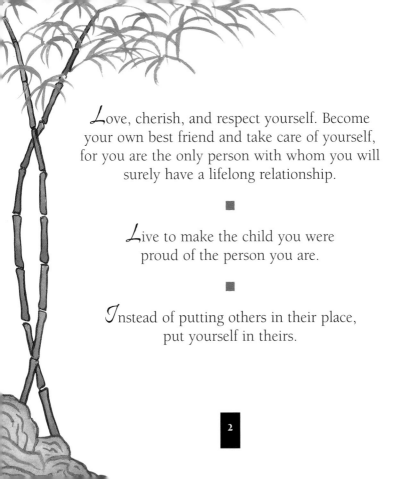

Love, cherish, and respect yourself. Become
your own best friend and take care of yourself,
for you are the only person with whom you will
surely have a lifelong relationship.

Live to make the child you were
proud of the person you are.

Instead of putting others in their place,
put yourself in theirs.

Experience is the only teacher
that gives the test first and the lesson later.

■

Apple, orange, and peach—
each, in its own way, is unique and valuable.
The same is true of people—each individual,
regardless of superficial differences,
is equally precious.

■

How much more joy we feel
when we seek not to make something of ourselves
but to make someone of ourselves.

$\mathcal{B}$e the kind of person
you wish to attract into your life.

◼

$\mathcal{N}$ecessary evils are never necessary
and always evil.

◼

$\mathcal{O}$ne who maintains a centered self
will not be self-centered.

◼

$\mathcal{I}$gnorance breeds fear.
Fear breeds hate.
Hate breeds violence.

*E*ducation breeds confidence.
Confidence breeds hope.
Hope breeds peace.

■

*T*he mind is a powerful and mysterious force.
It can make the best of the worst
and the worst of the best.

■

*A*s force begets resistance,
dialogue begets assistance.

■

*A*void allowing your sense of self to be
defined by the sum of your experiences.
Re-create yourself every day.

The truth is rarely obvious.

■

Having a child does not make you a parent, just as having a kitchen does not make you a chef.

■

A book is like a garden carried in one's pocket.
—Asian proverb

■

Know the difference between instinct and habit. Trust your instincts—question your habits.

$\mathcal{R}$ather than inherently good or evil,
people are essentially neutral and have
the choice of either creative
or destructive actions.

$\mathcal{K}$nowledge is of the past.
Wisdom is of the future.

$\mathcal{Y}$our actions speak your truth.

One may defeat a thousand
obstacles and adversaries, yet he
who defeats the enemies within
is the noblest victor.

— SHAKYAMUNI

$\mathcal{F}$ocus on the task at hand and give it your best.
Climb one mountain at a time,
starting with the one in front of you.

■

$\mathcal{D}$o something today to improve someone else's life.

■

$\mathcal{O}$ur relationships reflect our relationship
with ourselves.

Strength does not come from physical capacity. It comes from an indomitable will.

—*Mahatma Gandhi*

■

Figuring out what you truly want in life is difficult. Achieving it, by comparison, is easy.

■

There is always a way to get there from here.

Be concerned less with position
than being worthy of position.
Be concerned less with people knowing
you than developing qualities
worth knowing.

— CONFUCIUS

11

*I*nconspicuous spiritual treasures
such as self-respect, hope, wisdom, and
compassion are the greatest fortune. Without
these, conspicuous wealth
is trifling at best.

■

*P*eople of great character conduct
themselves with dignity, even in times
of crisis or despair—they do not complain,
panic, or lose hope even under the
most difficult circumstances.

$\mathcal{I}$t is a mistake to live your life thinking, "How perfect it would be if he or she did this or that" or "What a better place the world would be if this or that happened." It is imperative to base your life on yourself, to take responsibility for your own happiness.

—*Josei Toda*

$\mathcal{D}$esire is an unavoidable aspect of life. After all, to live one must desire to go on living. It is mastering one's desires, not eliminating them, that is most important.

The choices we make in thought, word, and deed
inevitably return to us in kind.

You cannot do right in one department of life while
occupied doing wrong in any other department.
Life is one indivisible whole.

—Mahatma Gandhi

The unity of those associated by mere authority,
power, or greed is ultimately weak and unstable.
In contrast, the unity of those united by the heart—
by bonds of respect, honesty, and compassion—
is strong and unshakable.

$\mathcal{P}$eople respect those who first show them respect.

■

$\mathcal{T}$here is no single recipe for a joyful life.
True happiness is ultimately an individual experience.

■

$\mathcal{W}$hen you look into your mind at any moment, you
perceive neither color nor form to verify that it exists.
Yet you still cannot say it does not exist, for many
differing thoughts continually occur to you. The mind,
like life itself, is an elusive reality that transcends both
the words and concepts of existence and nonexistence.
It is neither existence nor nonexistence, yet exhibits
the qualities of both. It is the mystic entity of the
Middle Way that is the reality of all things.

—*Nichiren*

Wise people always find a way to
bring out a smile.

One who lives life with passion is like a brightly
burning fire. A small, dim fire can easily be
extinguished by gusts of wind, but a large, bright
one will grow bigger as the wind grows stronger.
In the same way, the more obstacles a passionate
person encounters, the brighter and stronger
that person grows.

The birth of an idea in your mind and the birth of a
celestial star in distant space—both arise from the
same latent field of cosmic energy.

*F*ast ripe, fast rotten.

—*Japanese proverb*

■

*J*ust as the two sides of a coin are distinct yet inseparable, our lives have a physical, tangible dimension and a spiritual, intangible one. We may differentiate between body and mind, but at their most fundamental level, they are inseparable.

■

*H*old fast to your dreams. Never allow the enemy of self-doubt to destroy them.

*M*istaking subjective values for
objective truth leads to no good.

■

*I*t is better to see one time than to
hear one hundred times.

—*Mongolian proverb*

■

*T*hose who have not asked the question
are not ready to accept the answer.

■

*H*appy people adapt themselves to
circumstances as liquids adapt to containers.

*J*udge not the horse by his saddle.

—*Asian proverb*

◼

*W*hen we encounter criticism,
we make a choice: Accept it as an opportunity
to open our lives, or allow it to reinforce
our insecurities.

◼

*A*void becoming totally absorbed
in immediate realities—always remember
your ultimate dreams.

The Lotus Sutra, the ancient teaching that all people have enlightenment within them and are essentially equals, is a radical teaching. If it were not, then racial, sexual, and age discrimination, not to mention violence, terrorism, and war, would not exist.

■

Deluded minds discuss people.
Common minds discuss events.
Enlightened minds discuss ideas.

■

Nature makes no mistakes.

■

A parent's influence lasts forever.

—Japanese proverb

*Misfortune comes from
one's mouth and ruins one,
but fortune comes from
one's heart and makes
one worthy of respect.*

— NICHIREN

21

*T*rue creativity enhances one's existence
and contributes to the well-being of others
under all circumstances.

◼

*S*eek to understand your mistakes so that
you may never repeat them.

◼

*A*ll is changeable, nothing is constant.
—*Buddhist proverb*

◼

*H*ate is a cancer upon the soul.

*R*ather than defeat your enemies,
seek to transform them into allies.

■

*C*hange for the better requires effort.
Change for the worse needs none.

■

*I*f you seek enlightenment outside
yourself, any discipline or good deed will
be meaningless. For example, a poor man
cannot earn a penny just by counting his
neighbor's wealth, even if he does so
night and day.

—*Nichiren*

*W*rite the script of your own life,
rehearse it in your mind, then go out and
perform it to the best of your ability.

■

*P*eople often think of happiness as something
abstract, somehow separate from immediate reality.
The grass is never greener on the other side.
There is no other side.

■

*P*atience in one moment of anger can prevent
one hundred days of sorrow.

—Chinese proverb

*N*othing exists entirely alone; everything exists in relation to everything else. Where there is light, there is shadow; where there is birth, there is death; where there is open, there is closed; where there is one, there is other. By the same reasoning, where there is sadness, there is joy; where there is delusion, there is enlightenment.

*B*e truly whole, and all things will come to you.

—*Lao Tzu*

$\mathcal{T}$hose who can find joy in even the most difficult times will know a life without regret.

$\blacksquare$

$\mathcal{C}$ease all slander—both of yourself and of others.

$\blacksquare$

$\mathcal{J}$udge your actions by the value they create.

$\blacksquare$

$\mathcal{A}$ll of our thoughts, words, and deeds, whether positive or negative, are stored in the depths of our being, forming our karma, determining our fate.

*B*etter than one hundred years lived in vice is one single day lived in virtue. Better than one hundred years lived in ignorance is one single day lived in wisdom. Better than one hundred years lived in idleness and weakness is one single day lived with courage and powerful striving.

—*Shakyamuni*

*W*hen you do things simply to gain others' approval, you risk losing self-approval.

*R*emove the internal, emotional hooks that attract you to painful situations.

$\mathcal{W}$e should think of ourselves in community with everything around us at all times. We should regard people, animals, trees, rivers, even mountains in the same light as ourselves and realize that we all have much in common. Such thoughts cause us to imagine, "If I were in their (or its) place, how would I feel, or what would I do?" Sympathetic interaction naturally occurs when we regard other people and things in this way, as part of ourselves, as one of our own kind. When we place ourselves in the position of other people or objects and feel we share their experiences, positive actions arise for all concerned, both for people and for their environment.

—*Tsunesaburo Makiguchi*

Scientific and technological advances used against the greater good of humanity reflect a society whose technology has surpassed its spirituality.

◼

You have the potential to transform even the worst situation into a great opportunity.

◼

Always say what must be said.

◼

Seedlings change and become stalks. Stalks change and become rice. Rice changes and becomes a person. A person changes and becomes a Buddha.

—Nichiren

No one can give you abilities. For example, an Olympic athlete works with a trainer to develop her abilities, but the trainer only helps manifest what was inherent all along. Likewise, no one can give you happiness. At most, others simply help manifest the joy that was always within you.

Form is more important than pace.

Expect the best and prepare for the worst.

Focus less on treating the symptom than eliminating the cause.

*T*here is nothing softer or more yielding than
water, but none is superior to it in
overcoming the hard; it has no equal.
Weakness overcomes strength and gentleness
overcomes rigidity. Everyone knows this,
yet no one puts it into practice.

—*Lao Tzu*

*T*hink for yourself.

*B*e profoundly nonjudgmental.

*E*ven withered trees give prosperity
to the mountain.

—Japanese proverb

■

*I*f we wish to eliminate the negative,
unhealthy aspects of our lives, we would do
well to increase the positive, healthy ones.
Once strengthened, they will naturally help
us transform the negative.

■

*W*hat would your current frustrations
look like from the vantage point of the
final days of your life?

*T*ruth has the power to dispel the darkness of ignorance—just as a candle has the power to light a cave that has been dark for a million years.

■

*A*dversity is the raw material of indestructible happiness. That's why, when young, you ought to experience all sorts of hardships, even at a price.

—*Josei Toda*

■

*G*aining the respect of others is good. Gaining self-respect is better.

$\mathcal{T}$here is a bird that lives deep in the snowy mountains. Tortured by night's numbing cold, it cries that it will build a warm nest in the morning. Yet, when day breaks, it sleeps the day away, basking in the warmth of the sun. So it continues, crying vainly throughout its life. People are often the same, lamenting their circumstances yet passing by every opportunity to change.

$\mathcal{D}$evelop a profound belief in the universal law of cause and effect—the empowering conviction that we all ultimately direct our own lives.

If you want one year of prosperity, plant corn. If you want ten years of prosperity, grow trees. If you want one hundred years of prosperity, educate people.

—*Chinese proverb*

People who make the most of life
have no fear of death.

The more enlightening a teaching, the more difficult it is to believe and even more difficult to practice.

There are as many religions as there are individuals.

—*Mahatma Gandhi*

$\mathcal{I}$t is easy to be the person you have always been, for it requires no change, no self-reflection, and no growth. It may appear that changing yourself requires giving up something. In reality, there is no need to give up anything—you simply add to what has been.

$\mathcal{C}$reate a mission statement for your life.

$\mathcal{Y}$ou cannot carve rotten wood.

—Confucius

$\mathcal{J}$oy is character plus a good philosophy.

One should neither be overly jubilant when flattered
nor overly distressed when criticized.

The question isn't to whom you are attracted but why.

Worldly fame and profit are mere baubles of your
present existence, and arrogance and prejudice are ties
that will fetter you in the next.

—Nichiren

There is no substitute for hard work.

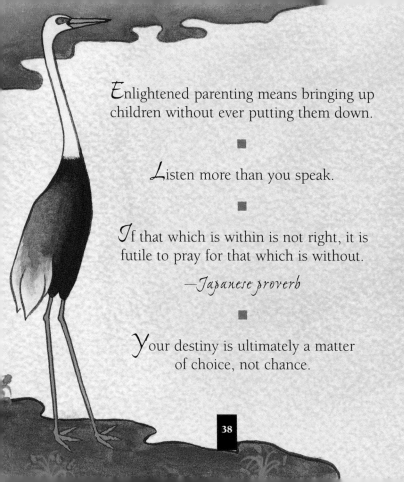

Enlightened parenting means bringing up children without ever putting them down.

Listen more than you speak.

If that which is within is not right, it is futile to pray for that which is without.

—*Japanese proverb*

Your destiny is ultimately a matter of choice, not chance.

*W*isdom, courage, and compassion—
three essential elements of a noble life.

■

*T*alent comes from the inner and is shaped
by the outer. Genius comes from the inner
and shapes the outer.

■

*W*ise people understand even unspoken words.

■

*I*t is better to be unknown and accomplish much
than to be known and accomplish little.

Like beautiful flowers of
color and perfume are the fruitful words
of the virtuous, who speak and then do as they
say. Although the perfume of flowers carries
not against the wind, not even the fragrant
sandalwood, or oleander, or jasmine, the
perfume of the virtuous travels against the
wind and reaches around the world.

—*Shakyamuni*

As water carves through stone, those who
persevere will win.

The essence of education is not to transfer knowledge; it is to guide the learning process, to put responsibility for study into the students' own hands. It is not the piecemeal merchandising of information; it is the bestowal of keys that allow people to unlock the vault of knowledge on their own. It does not consist of pilfering the intellectual property amassed by others through no additional effort of one's own; it would rather place people on their own path of discovery and invention.

—Tsunesaburo Makiguchi

One word from a person who is trusted carries more weight than ten thousand from someone who is not.

*R*ecognizing your faults is as difficult
and beneficial as acknowledging your
adversary's virtues.

■

*C*ultivation of tolerance for other faiths will impart
to us a truer understanding of our own.

—*Mahatma Gandhi*

■

*W*e achieve relative to what we believe.

■

*A*nger is only one letter short of *danger.*

There once was a baby circus elephant who couldn't break free from her leg chain, though she tried and tried. Eventually, she gave up. Years later, she still had that little chain around her leg. Although she was strong enough to break free, she had long since accepted that she could not. Emotional chains, after all, are the hardest to break.

You are your own master. Could anyone else be your master? When you have gained control over yourself, you have found a master of rare value.

—Buddhist proverb

Always act upon a generous impulse.

$\mathcal{D}$on't belittle—be big.

◼

$\mathcal{I}$n thinking, keep to the simple. In conflict, be fair
and generous. In governing, don't try to control.
In work, do what you enjoy. In family life,
be completely present.

—$\mathcal{L}$ao $\mathcal{T}$zu

◼

$\mathcal{F}$oolish criticism, an honor.
Foolish praise, a disgrace.

◼

$\mathcal{M}$any a have and have-not of today are a
did and did-not of yesterday.

$\mathcal{F}$ocus on the positive, for what you
focus on increases.

One does not throw away gold because the bag
that holds it is dirty; one does not ignore the
sandalwood trees because of the foul odor of the
eranda trees around them; and one does not refuse
to gather lotuses because the pond in the valley
where they grow is unclean.

—Nichiren

You are the person you are when no one is looking.

Of two evils, choose neither.

*T*he rarest form of intelligence
is common sense.

*E*ven dust can become a mountain.

—*Japanese proverb*

*O*ne who works with you is equal
to ten who work for you.

A moment is to one's day
as a day is to one's life.

$\mathcal{I}$f you want to understand your present circumstances, review your past actions. If you want to know your future circumstances, examine your present actions.

■

$\mathcal{T}$rue friendship is stronger than stone.

—*Mongolian proverb*

■

$\mathcal{L}$ive for this day as if there were no other. Today *is* tomorrow.

■

$\mathcal{P}$eople don't stop enjoying life when they become old; people become old when they stop enjoying life.

Great achievements involve great risks.

■

Consider others as yourself.

—*Shakyamuni*

■

Strive most to understand what you fear most.

■

Talent seeks to become something.
Genius seeks to become someone.

■

When we stop to think more,
we stop to thank more.

48

The universe is life itself. When we die, our lives melt back into the greater life of the universe and are nowhere to be found, much like the interval of sleep when our minds are seemingly nowhere. Just as we resume our mental activities from the previous day upon awakening, so too are we born with our karma from previous existences. In this way, just as we sleep and wake, we are born and die, maintaining an eternal cycle of life.

—Josei Toda

Know-how is good; know-why is better; know-when is best.

$\mathcal{W}$e mold our habits at first,
but our habits mold us in the end.

$\mathcal{D}$on't believe those who would hold you back.

$\mathcal{F}$lowing water never goes bad.

—*Chinese proverb*

$\mathcal{W}$hen you have more to live for,
you can always live with less.

$\mathcal{L}$earn to say no.

Birth and death are not two different states
but different aspects of the same state.

—*Mahatma Gandhi*

■

Happiness does not mean "absence of problems."
There has never been, nor will there ever be,
a life free from problems. It is not the presence
of problems but how we tackle them that
determines the quality of our lives.

■

Obstacles help us uncover the difference
between what we truly want and what
we merely think we want.

Wealth and popularity gained through unsavory
means are but clouds floating in the sky.

—*Confucius*

Money only buys what can be bought.

The difference between an opinion and a conviction
is that you hold one while the other holds you.

Live lightly on the Earth.

—*Tsunesaburo Makiguchi*

$\mathcal{A}$ good time to study human nature
is when you are alone.

$\mathcal{E}$liminate the poisons of selfishness,
ignorance, and violence from your life.

$\mathcal{I}$ron, when heated in flames and pounded,
becomes a fine sword. Worthies and sages
are likewise tested by abuse.

—Nichiren

*M*arriage rites will not right what is already wrong.

■

*O*ne does not win by making others lose.

■

*L*ife will give you back what you give out.

■

*T*o observe evil acts and do nothing to stop them is to share responsibility for such acts.

—*Tsunesaburo Makiguchi*

Control your work; don't let it control you.

The question isn't whom you love but how.

Expecting someone else to make you happy
will ultimately have the opposite effect.

Blind faith is no faith.

$\mathcal{B}$e a lamp unto yourself. Rely only on yourself.

—Buddhist proverb

$\mathcal{O}$ne who is afraid to ask is afraid to learn.

$\mathcal{C}$ultivate tolerance, even of the intolerant.

$\mathcal{A}$ll things are essentially neutral, neither positive
nor negative, but gain positive or negative value
depending on perception and circumstances.
Anger is generally considered negative.
Anger, however, can also be righteous when,
for example, aimed at correcting injustice.

What we are today comes from our thoughts of yesterday, and our present thoughts build our life of tomorrow. Our life is the creation of our mind.

—*Shakyamuni*

We often see others as we see ourselves. Those caught up in deceit and posturing tend to mistrust even the well-meaning actions of others. In contrast, a person of integrity tends to trust that others are the same, even when they are not.

Someone is always doing what someone else said couldn't be done.

*W*e think and behave within the boundaries of
our beliefs. The key, then, to fulfilling our
potential without limitations is to master
our beliefs, to master our minds.

A truly wise person will not be carried away
by any of the eight winds: prosperity, decline,
disgrace, honor, praise, censure,
suffering, pleasure.

—*Nichiren*

*C*hange in the quality of life for one group of
humanity, for better or worse, inevitably leads to
a change in the quality of life for all humanity.

*A*void living the life your unhappy experiences
would have you live.

■

*T*he sage puts himself last and finds himself
in the foremost place.

—*Lao Tzu*

■

*O*ne who grabs much grasps little.

■

A truly civilized society is one in which each
individual cultivates the inner power to defeat
his or her negativity, with or without
external pressure.

$\mathcal{T}$here once lived a powerful king who undertook an expedition to conquer foreign lands. His wise counselor asked him, "Great King, to what purpose do you set out on this endeavor?"

"To become master of Asia," the king replied.

"And then what?" asked the counselor.

"I shall invade Arabia," said the king.

"And after that?"

"I shall conquer Europe and Africa; and finally, when the whole world is under me, I shall rest and live at ease."

To this the wise counselor retorted, "But what keeps you from resting and living at ease here and now, if that is all you want? You could settle down this very day without the trouble and risks."

$\mathcal{A}$ few kind words can warm three winter months.

—*Japanese proverb*

$\mathcal{T}$here are two things you should never worry about—
things you can help, and things you can't.

$\mathcal{S}$top complaining.

$\mathcal{I}$t is all right not to like everyone.

$\mathcal{T}$urn your face to the sun and shadows
will only fall behind you.

—*Asian proverb*

$\mathcal{Y}$ou determine whether your experiences
make you bitter or better.

$\mathcal{W}$ithout wisdom, knowledge can be more
harmful than ignorance.

$\mathcal{I}$t takes far more courage to go against custom than to go against law.

■

$\mathcal{S}$hakyamuni was once asked, "If life is precious, yet all people live by killing and eating other living things, which things may we kill and which must we not?"

Shakyamuni replied, "It is enough to kill the will to kill."

■

$\mathcal{W}$herever you go, go with all your heart.

—Confucius

*C*reate something of value today.

■

A change in surroundings
will not help you unless you have first
made a change in yourself.

■

*I*nvest more in your inner development
than your outward appearance.

Keep your thoughts positive, because your thoughts become your words. Keep your words positive, because your words become your behavior. Keep your behavior positive, because your behavior becomes your habits. Keep your habits positive, because your habits become your values. Keep your values positive, because your values become your destiny.

— MAHATMA GANDHI

*T*he Buddhist concept of the Ten Worlds illustrates the changing conditions of life that human beings experience on a daily basis. While a person can experience any or all of these on a daily basis, a single life-condition tends to dominate:

Buddhahood—enlightened, altruistic, unshakable happiness

Bodhisattva—devotion to the happiness of others

Realization—seeking happiness through direct experience

Learning—seeking happiness through the teachings of others

Heaven—intense elation from fulfilled desires

Humanity—reasonable, logical behavior

Anger—arrogant, ego-driven behavior

Animality—bullying the weak, ingratiating the strong

Hunger—fixation by insatiable desires

Hell—hopeless, destructive, overwhelming suffering

*C*ompassion is a universal medicine
for humanity's ills.

■

*T*he deeper the roots, the more luxuriant
the branches. The farther the source,
the longer the stream.

—*Nichiren*

■

*T*here is no greater aid on the road to happiness
than a true friend.

■

*M*aster your past in the present,
or the past will master your future.

The lotus flower blooms most beautifully
from the deepest and thickest mud.

■

Enlightenment, or true happiness, is not a
transcendental state. It is a condition of broad
wisdom, boundless energy, and good fortune
wherein we each shape our own destiny, find
fulfillment in daily activities, and come to
understand our ultimate purpose in life.

—*Josei Toda*

■

Refuse to lower yourself to the level
of your antagonist.

*T*here's a time for everything,
but most people can't wait.

◼

*Y*our teacher can open the door,
but you must enter by yourself.

—Chinese proverb

◼

*B*e true to yourself. Live your life in a way
that best suits your unique identity.

◼

*B*ias and bigotry arise from feelings
of insecurity and inadequacy.

Doing your best when no one is paying attention will help you more than standing in the spotlight.

To not advance is to retreat.

—Tsunesaburo Makiguchi

One of these days is none of these days.

Make time to care for yourself.

*E*verything that people say or do is ultimately
rooted in the belief that those actions
will lead them to happiness.

◼

*T*he person who confesses ignorance shows it once;
the person who conceals it shows it many times.

—*Japanese proverb*

◼

*T*ruly brave is the person who is strong when
standing alone.

◼

*O*ur happiness is determined more by our perception
of what happens in life than by what actually happens.

*O*nce upon a time, a small bird named Tasoo lived in a vast jungle. One hot summer day, a terrible wildfire erupted and the flames devoured many trees and animals living in the jungle. Other birds flew high into the sky and far away to safety, but Tasoo couldn't bear to leave her precious jungle home to burn. Day and night, she flew with all her might back and forth to the river, filling her tiny beak with water to drop on the raging fires. Tasoo's rare heart of courage and unshakable determination moved the heavenly gods to shed tears, and a great rain poured down upon the jungle, extinguishing the flames. And so it is that even the smallest actions of a determined spirit can change the world.

*W*hen the student is ready, the teacher will appear.

—*Buddhist proverb*

❖

A great mentor is one who aims for others' ability to surpass his own.

❖

*E*veryone fails sometimes, but no one is ever a failure.

❖

*L*et go of anger—it is an acid that burns away the delicate layers of your happiness.

*E*agles don't chase flies.

—*Mongolian proverb*

■

*Y*our actions are simultaneously the result of past karma and the creation of new karma. Action creates memory, and that memory creates desire. Desire produces further action, which continues the cycle of karma. To be aware of this reality and to master your actions are the keys to creating the karma of happiness.

■

*R*emember your debts of gratitude.

You do wrong when you do nothing.

◾

It is better to have a heart without words
than words without a heart.

—*Mahatma Gandhi*

◾

To change our lives, we must first
change our minds.

◾

True success is measured less by quantity
than by quality.

Life appears throughout the universe wherever
and whenever conditions are right, much like waves
appear in the ocean as windy conditions arise.
As a wave is simply an individual expression of the
greater ocean, so too are we expressions of
the greater life of the universe.

A compassionate spirit to help others, even those we
may dislike, gives rise to the deepest wisdom.

If you care anything about your personal security,
you should first of all pray for order and tranquility
throughout the four quarters of the land.

—*Nichiren*

$\mathcal{A}$ nation that desires peace
must prepare for peace.

◼

$\mathcal{G}$iving of oneself is the surest path to personal growth.

◼

$\mathcal{T}$he wise leave aside fleeting pleasures, looking
instead to far-reaching happiness.

—Shakyamuni

◼

$\mathcal{K}$eep the wisdom gained from painful experiences
and let go of the rest. Otherwise, risk the wisdom
diminishing while the pain lingers.

There once was a woman who lost her child to disease. Crazy with grief, she stumbled through the city begging for medicine to bring her child back. When she came upon the Buddha, he told her he would give her the medicine she needed. He asked her to find a poppy from a house where no one had lost a loved one. In her quest, she found there was not even one such home. She realized that death is a fact of life, and that she was not alone in her grief. In this way, the Buddha awakened her wisdom, restoring peace to her heart.

■

Fall seven times, stand up eight.

—Japanese proverb

*T*ime spent feeling sorry for oneself
is time wasted.

*T*he nature of *Good* may be defined as anything
promoting harmonious coexistence, empathy, and
compassion. *Evil,* on the other hand, promotes
divisiveness. It may be thought of as anything that
divides person from person, nation from nation,
or humanity from nature.

*H*umanity is one tribe.

$\mathcal{T}$he higher the position a leader holds in the political, the religious, or any realm, the more humble he or she should become.

■

$\mathcal{A}$ dynamic life is a constant struggle against complacency.

■

$\mathcal{L}$oneliness is a choice.

■

$\mathcal{I}$f there were one word that could act as a standard of conduct for one's entire life, perhaps it would be *thoughtfulness*.

—*Confucius*

People who live lives of justice
invariably face adversity.

■

Beware of articulate fools.

■

In all affairs of life, at every moment,
we have a choice.

■

Humans cannot create matter. We can, however,
create value. Creating value is, in fact, the essence of
our humanity. When we praise people for their
strength of character, we are actually acknowledging
their ability to create value.

—Tsunesaburo Makiguchi

*E*verything you need to break unhealthy cycles of behavior is within you.

◼

*I*n the general sense, to have faith means to establish one's awareness of true self—to realize that the infinite dignity of the universe and the nature of one's life are the same; to recognize that indestructible happiness exists right here and now within oneself. In this light, to have faith means to cherish and develop the potential of one's own precious life.

◼

*N*onviolence requires much more courage than violence.

—*Mahatma Gandhi*

There are three kinds of law: social and
moral law, or culturally acceptable behavior;
civil and criminal law, or legally accepted behavior;
and universal law, or cause and effect.
We may avoid the consequences of breaking
the first two, but never the third.

That which governs your destiny is found
in your own heart.

We don't agree with the opinions of others;
we simply agree with our own opinions
expressed by others.

*T*here is always a piece of fortune in misfortune.

—*Japanese proverb*

*O*ur attitudes and perceptions are colored by our memories of past experiences, which form our biases and predispositions. Our current viewpoint, then, is simply a reflection of our ever-changing memory.

*W*hat irritates us most about others is often what we dislike most about ourselves.

There are three types of causes: thoughts, words, and deeds. Of the three, thoughts are the most powerful, for words and deeds arise only from thoughts.

The person worth listening to is often the quietest person.

—Japanese proverb

Manifest the courage to follow your talents wherever they lead.

$\mathcal{P}$eace is possible only when reason rules.

—*Asian proverb*

■

$\mathcal{B}$ecome a revisionist of your own history.
Go back into your halls of memory and find the
courage to view those experiences again—only this
time through the clear vision of retrospection.
Give yourself the answers you did not have then,
learn what you once failed to learn, and allow
yourself and others to have been wrong.
Then let it go. When you do this, you will feel
a sense of boundless, joyful freedom.

■

$\mathcal{S}$eek to find the positive in everyone.

$\mathcal{A}$n unhappy person and a happy one will have
different perceptions of the same circumstances.
The difference lies not in the circumstances
but in the two states of life.

$\mathcal{B}$irth and death, appearance and disappearance, gain
and loss, existence and extinction—all are essential
and everlasting processes.

$\mathcal{G}$uessing is cheap; guessing wrong is expensive.

—*Chinese proverb*

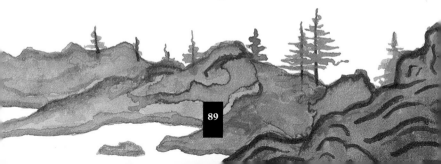

*I*n debate, remember that you and the point you are making are two different things.

■

*A*s spring water rushes through open earth, so happiness flows through open lives.

■

*L*et go of hate—people consumed by it often become exactly what they once hated.

■

*I*ntuition transcends the limitations of reason.

When we are upset, it's easy to blame others. The true cause of our feelings, however, is within us. For example, imagine yourself as a glass of water. Now, imagine past negative experiences as sediment at the bottom of your glass. Next, think of others as spoons. When stirred, the sediment clouds your water. It may appear that the spoon caused the water to cloud—but if there were no sediment, the water would remain clear. The key, then, is to identify our sediment and actively work to remove it.

—Josei Toda

Until we learn the lessons inherent in unpleasant experiences, they will continue to hold power over us, and we will feel compelled to repeat them.

$\mathcal{T}$he wise are sensitive to right and wrong; they cease doing anything as soon as they see that it is wrong, and they appreciate those who call their attention to it.

■

$\mathcal{A}$pparent distinctions exist only in our minds. For example, in the sky there is no distinction of east and west. People create such distinctions and then believe them to be true. We do the same in everyday life—making distinctions, such as "us" and "them," where none exist and then believing them to be real.

■

$\mathcal{W}$inter always turns to spring.

—Nichiren

When we enter a house, we first notice the interior and only later look out the windows. In like manner, our mind's eye cannot correctly see the external before it correctly sees the internal.

■

Both water and oil become round in a round glass and square in a square one. Water and oil have no shape in and of themselves. The same is true of good and evil. Good and evil actions may take the same shape, yet the wise can perceive the difference.

■

The means by which an end is reached must exemplify the value of the end itself.

*W*hat is possible for one is possible for all.

—*Mahatma Gandhi*

◼

*O*ne's schooling is no indication of one's wisdom.

◼

*G*reed arises from an inaccurate perception
of one's true desires.

◼

*W*hen someone's character is not clear to you,
look at that person's friends.

—*Japanese proverb*

94

Strive to achieve whatever you think you cannot,
for it is on the path toward your impossible
dream that you will find what you truly seek.

■

Doing the right thing is easy—
knowing the right thing to do is difficult.

■

More valuable than treasures
in a storehouse are treasures of the body,
and the treasures of the heart
are the most valuable of all.

—*Nichiren*

HISTORIC FIGURES

■

CONFUCIUS (551–479 B.C.E.)—CHINA
Founder of Confucianism

Also known as K'ung Fu Tzu. Recognized as China's premier teacher, both chronologically and in importance, Confucius based his school of thought on the most enduring and universal aspects of human experience, such as family, friendship, education, community, and so on, guaranteeing his teachings' relevance for generations to come. Over his lifetime Confucius also edited what were to become the Chinese classics, including poetry, music, history, extensive commentary on the *Book of Changes*, and annals that chronicled events of the Lu court.

Mahatma Gandhi (1869–1948)—India
Social Reformer, Spiritual Leader

Born Mohandas K. Gandhi, later given the honorific title Mahatma (Great Spirit) by his supporters. Raised in India, Gandhi studied law in London and later worked for twenty years to improve human rights in South Africa. After returning to India in 1914, he led the struggle for independence against Britain. His belief in the power of tolerance and nonviolent protest was never shaken. As a result, India's independence in 1947 was heralded not as a military triumph but as a victory of indomitable human will. Gandhi was assassinated on January 30, 1948.

Tsunesaburo Makiguchi (1871–1944)—Japan
Humanist Philosopher, Educational Reformer

Founder of the Soka Gakkai (Value-Creating Society), a Buddhist peace movement established in 1930, comprising at the time mostly reformist educators. Makiguchi strove to introduce a more humanistic, student-centered approach to education. During World War II he staunchly opposed Japan's military government and was imprisoned in 1943 as a "thought criminal." Despite severe conditions and interrogation, he never retreated from his beliefs. On November 18, 1944, the anniversary of his founding of the Soka Gakkai, he died in prison at the age of seventy-three.

NICHIREN (1222–1282)—JAPAN
Buddhist Philosopher, Religious Reformer

Also known as Nichiren Daishonin. Nichiren established the Buddhist practice of chanting *Nam-myoho-renge-kyo* to "polish one's inner mirror" of enlightenment. Through his study of the Lotus Sutra, he became convinced of the inherent enlightenment and equality of all people—

revolutionary concepts for thirteenth-century Japan and unpopular with the ruling class. He fearlessly remonstrated throughout his life with priests and politicians who continually condemned him as a traitor, banishing him twice and once nearly beheading him for his reformist teachings.

SHAKYAMUNI (CIRCA 600–500 B.C.E.)— INDIA AND NEPAL
Founder of Buddhism

Also known as Siddhartha Gautama or Shakyamuni Buddha. Born a prince of the Shakya clan, Shakyamuni renounced his royal status to begin a religious quest, reportedly at age twenty-nine. He wished to find a spiritual solution to free humanity from the four universal sufferings of birth, sickness, old age, and death. After seven years he is said to have seated himself at the foot of a large pipal tree, fallen into a deep meditation, and soon thereafter attained enlightenment to the ultimate reality of life and the universe. Many Buddhists consider the Lotus Sutra his ultimate teaching.

JOSEI TODA (1900–1958)—JAPAN
Reformist Educator, Buddhist Leader

Founder of the Soka Gakkai (Value-Creating Society), together with his mentor, Tsunesaburo Makiguchi. Through his Buddhist studies Toda came to believe that enlightenment is inherent in life itself and therefore attainable by all people. He met with severe harassment and persecution during World War II for his unyielding commitment to human rights. He was imprisoned by the militarist Japanese government in 1943 on charges of blasphemy. After the war Toda and his successor, Daisaku Ikeda, rebuilt the Soka Gakkai, which now has twelve million members in 180 nations.

Lao Tzu (circa 600–500 b.c.e.)—China
Founder of Taoism

Credited with writing the *Tao Te Ching* (*The Way and Its Power*), the foundation of Taoism. Most scholars believe Lao Tzu was the imperial court's archive keeper and an older contemporary of Confucius. When he was eighty Lao Tzu set out for the country's western border, where a soldier asked him to record his teachings before leaving. Lao Tzu then composed in five thousand characters the *Tao Te Ching*. Some scholars feel that Lao Tzu is only a legend and that the *Tao Te Ching* is actually a compilation of writings by several Taoists using the collective pen name Lao Tzu.

To learn more about this book and its author please visit:
www.tarogold.com